To Sc

Donald Davie

TO SCORCH OR FREEZE

POEMS ABOUT THE SACRED

CARCANET

First published in 1988 by
Carcanet Press Limited
208–212 Corn Exchange Buildings
Manchester M4 3BQ

British Library Cataloguing in Publication Data

Davie, Donald
To scorch or freeze: poems about the sacred.
I. Title
821′. 914

ISBN 0-85635-825-8

The publisher acknowledges financial assistance
from the Arts Council of Great Britain

Typeset in 10pt Palatino by Bryan Williamson, Manchester
Printed in England by SRP Ltd, Exeter

Contents

The Thirty-ninth Psalm, Adapted

I said to myself: "That's enough.
Your life-style is no model.
Keep quiet about it, and while
you're about it, be less overt."

I held my tongue, I said nothing;
no, not comfortable words.
"Writing-block", it's called;
very discomfiting.

Not that I had no feelings.
I was in a fever.
And while I seethed,
abruptly I found myself speaking:

"Lord, let me know my end,
and how long I have to live;
let me be sure
how long I have to live.

One-finger you poured me;
what does it matter to you
to know my age last birthday?
Nobody's life has purpose.

Something is casting a shadow
on everything we do;
and in that shadow nothing,
nothing at all, comes true.

(We make a million, maybe;
and who, not nobody but
who, gets to enjoy it?)

Now, what's left to be hoped for?
Hope has to be fixed on you.
Excuse me my comforting words
in a tabloid column for crazies.

I held my tongue, and also
I discontinued my journals.
(They accumulated; who
in any event would read them?)

Now give me a chance. I am
burned up enough at your pleasure.
It is all very well, we deserve it.
But shelved, not even with mothballs?

Hear my prayer, O Lord,
and please to consider my calling:
it commits me to squawking
and running off at the mouth."

Benedictus

Importunately
inopportune,

blessed is he that cometh in
the name of the

splendour between
ice and pearl cover in
the clockless distance,

flying the polar route as
we did in those days
                                        (We have been
                                                    modern
                                                          so long!)

Poet Redeemed & Dead

Feeling good, green light, the earthly paradise,
where is it, poet? Not
in this or that inn, on this or that fell, supplying
this or that cheese, but in
old age, innoxious,
knowing its guilts and not
forgiving itself but assured,
you knew how, of pardon.

Attar of Roses

The mind (the soul) is not
a ghost in the box of the body or brain, although it
excusably seems so. For instance at times
recalling our priests who instructed us in
The Resurrection of the Body

– at Judgement Day, the cadavers out of their coffins,
boxes emerging from boxes! What nonsense,
he blindingly observed –

who was himself, it may be said, a little
fleshy, more than a little coarse,
and maladroit with it, not to say uncivil.

What female parishioner wants him resurrected,
if so in what shape, and for what fanciful purpose?
But all the same, do we live in a nest of boxes,
the nubs of ourselves, so tiny, secreted in
the innermost, most reclusive, most
cramped of the boxes? If not

we have to believe in, we already believe in,
the resurrection of the body

which is not a box, but a main
sweet-smelling part of what the box encloses.

Sing Unto The Lord a New Song

Cheerfulness in lordly
leisure; and
holiness in thunder and high wind.

The lordly thunder
cleaves out flakes of fire.

The lightning uncovers the woods,
making the roe-deer calve
untimely in the bracken.

It is the holiness thunders.

Do not ask for the storm to ease.
Spirits rise, the longer it goes on.
Imagine Him yawning, hear Him
crack His joints as He stretches,
magisterial!

Praise the Lord upon the harp,
sing to him on the damnable steel guitar!

"So make them melt as the dishousèd snail"

"or as the embryo, whose vital band
breaks ere it holds".
                                        As we grow old, the basics
(as you might say) emerge
with an uncanny force:
we and our siblings each day more alike.

"The ungodly are froward
                        even from their mothers wombe;
as soon as they be borne they go astray;
born and perverted in one day,
lie, flatter, and betray."

It seems there are such doomed creatures;
morally
spina bifida. But

as we grow old the features of one
or the other parent show up in the mirror
frightening and affecting, and we can

under the heavenly justice

be equalled with slug or snail but
hardly with the aborted
almost-brother who would have
been so like us. The psalmist goes too far:

Best not be born, he means.

Better be born a snail,
or lying and betraying,
so you be born.

God Saves The King

To the chief Chanters
upon the dumb Dove in far places:
    either your brows are knitted,
    or you whinny and smirk, such teasers,
    you take such pains.

Far the places
and you are in their hands
who feast on squabs.

But care for that other way
of being debonair:

the sauntering monarch's, David's,
whose vigorous warmth did variously impart
to wives and concubines, to chariot-wheels,
to realms and officers,

religious faith; that is,
light spareness, unconcern.

Meteorologist, September

We shall break out
into the mention of God's great goodness,
and the abruptness of it.

The year goes round,
yes, but with what ructions!
The violence of the turns!
Why else are Revolutions always bloody
except that seasonal change is the type of them,
calamitous though foreseen?

At the autumnal equinox
gales.
        Though the belief is
"unsupported by observation",
rationality and
superstition alike require it:
God does not make His changes
without some pother.

His steady counsels change the face
of the declining year.

He flings gross icy gobbets from His hand –
fire and hail, snow and vapours,
wind and storm, subduing the land.

By Him the rain
supples the clods of indurated acres.

His whirled-down snows are laid
like bleaching wool beside the streams
to clad the tender blade.

Breath steams on the sharpened air.
And who so hardy as to bear
the quickness of His frost?

He blows a cold too strong for strongest things.

His power declare,
you empty air,
and snow out of nowhere, suddenly.

Vengeance Is Mine, Saith The Lord

You that would bite the whole pie and
mell with the pack, yet pout yourself ill-used,

you have committed crimes
against the innocent for
no profit but self-promotion.
Mouse has a broken back by
the coarsest cheese in the larder.

The creaking scissors and the penman's knife,
derailed from their proper business, will do justice
in a *collage* of your cruelties.
"The children
wore their cagoules, but these were mortar-bombs."

In the casinos most were vacuous, some
were fleshy and flaming, some profuse, some grasping,
far from Beirut.
Though I
address the mute, He hears, will testify.

Standings

"One Law for the Lion and Ox is Oppression."

For Woman & Man, for White & Black, for Bent &
Straight, for Sick & Sane
one Law is Oppression?

Across the Albion of William Blake,
a tesselation of ghettos,
the traveller beds down at night in
a Fabian or Lesbian canton, in
a Rastafarian or Israelite republic,
crossing from jurisdiction
to jurisdiction, never
tyrannised, never chastened.

Divers waights and divers measures are
abomination to the Lord.

There is not the psychiatrist's truth,
and then the poet's;
the white man's truth, then the black's.

The Lord admits diversity of gifts,
but not disparity.
We need to know where we stand.

Happy the man or the brute
who stands corrected,
stands like that, helped like that to stand,
enabled to,

hungry for judgement always.

Church Militant

In the day of the mustering of thine army,
thy people shall be willing:

the young men come to thee as dew,
the dew of thy youth comes unto thee.

From everlasting to
God knows . . . But this is history,
vouched for over and over:

as dew from the sources of the morning
sparkles upon the grasses,
the Commander recruits His youth
repeatedly, the converts crowd
the rail and His army masses.

Always they all passed muster;
always they were triumphant.
Always, you would have it,
they were insincere or deluded.

Curtains!

The Lord is King, be the people
never so impatient; He
sitteth between the Cherubim,
let the earth stir as it will.

"And what if I
fall down and die?
Can the sun go down at noon?
His years are one perpetual day,
and shall His children die so soon?"

Soon is not soon. This earth grows old,
Auriga and the Bear shall be folded away
like the costumes for Act One.
The star-scene shifts at His command.
The Twins, the Southern Cross, the Scales
flap on their hangers, ungainly.

"Stars, far things..."
But in the reach of His arm.

For He is One, still One;
the clock-hand wavers, uncertain.
Whatever the next production, you
are there when the curtain rises.

Auriga and the Bear,
The Twins, the Southern Cross
show that He is there
for ever, as they are not.

"And Our Eternal Home"

Time like an ever-rolling stream
bears not its sons away,
but its own segments, years and days.

They fly forgotten, not as dream,
as thought:
        "We have spent our years
        as it were a thought",

        few and short, or long and many
        according as we think of them.
        Keeping a tally is
        little to the purpose.

"So teach us to number our days..."
Certainly number amazes.
Numberlessness however
astonishes mathematicians
more than the innumerate; they
live with it every day.

Suppose we counted our birthdays
by the difficult measure, *stasis?*

Fill us with gladness betimes
(betimes!) and we shall be glad
all our days,
seeing the calendar is
an illusion – and blissful at that,
if you can face it squarely.

Zion

Mired in it! Stuck in the various
rust-coloured, dove-coloured, yellowish
or speckled muds of history, you mistook
clarity, the dayspring from on high,
for a satisfaction of art, or the condition
of addressing the untutored.
(As you never
did, they were otherwise tutored.)

Once, stuck in the mud by the Capitol,
you thought of the ninth buried city,
Richmond, Montgomery, what you had built them for,

of Troy, and of Rome, of Richmond, of Rome, not Zion;

of Troy, of Troynovant, of London,
the West Country, sometimes Geneva,
never of Zion;

of New Caledonia, New
Amsterdam, New Zealand,
Rome (Georgia), other Romes
and Athenses of the North,

New Delhi, Athens, Syracuse, not Zion.

Tutored in computer-processing,
still they may learn of Zion.

Trained in marketing techniques they
may discern in that murk the clarity
of a city not built on seven hills,

not guarding a river-crossing
nor plugging a gap in the mountains.

Unskilled in Islamic culture, they
may still make a Mecca of Zion.

Having heard or not heard of Lindisfarne, Iona,
are not the lot of us pilgrims?

The variegation of muds,
the iridescences,
constitute for some
in youth a passion,
in age a distraction from boredom

which, if designedly aimless
for long enough, merits the name of
Zion or some say Eden.

Felicity's Fourth Order

Men of business, of pleasure,
too often men of learning,
must not be left at leisure.

Their satisfaction is
forgetting themselves in work.
Nothing else is diverting.

Concupiscence, though of knowledge,
is a debauch, and only
an art against thinking of ends.

Vacancy however, if
careful of its ends but
aimless, may earn the Fourth Order:

"Being gathered into their chambers,
and guarded by angels in profound quiet,
they understand the rest that they enjoy."

Put Not Your Trust in Princes

Let them give up the ghost, then there is nothing but dust
left of their presumptions we were fools enough to trust.

Pin no more hopes on them, nor the promissory collective;
the light at that end of the tunnel is glass, the credit
delusive.

In the presence of the authorities we spent our days
turning our caps in our hands, and the manful,
inveigling phrase.

We combed our sparse hair in the mornings (silvered,
we observed).
We regarded our consort sleeping, whom we had
shabbily served.

They are lost among the histories, names of world-mastering
heroes:
this, the peace-fixer; that, the cuckolded smith of Infernos.

Having the sceptre no more, no more the ambiguous terms
of an unbelieved spokesman parade them; their press-men
too feed worms.

Their Rectitude Their Beauty

"The angels rejoice in
the excellencies of God;
the inferior creatures in
His goodness; sinners only
in His forgiveness."

His polar oppositions;
the habitable zones,
His clemencies; and
His smiling divagations,
uncovenanted mercies,

who turned the hard rock into a standing water
and the flint-stone into a springing well.

The voice of joy and health is in the dwellings of the
righteous;
my eyes are running with rheum
from looking for that health

in one who has stuck by
His testimonies;
who has delighted in
His regimen; who has run
the circuit of His requirements;
whose songs in the caravanserai
have been about His statutes,

not to deserve nor observe them
(having done neither) but
for the angelic reason:

their rectitude,
their beauty.

Except The Lord Build The House

A son of the degrees,
of the gradations,
the steps to the temple...

There is no need to insist;
it is enough to name them.

For Zion is a city
uniform in itself,
compact together.

Why are you so strenuous, my soul?
Vain to get up early,
to sit up late,
to bolt your bread in a hurry.

Short be your sleep and coarse your fare
in vain. The Lord shall turn
the key in the captivity of Zion,
and all go like a dream.

The grass grows over the ruins of Eblis,
nobody's hayfield;
you are loitering there, or studying
hard (you are a hard
loiterer) but no one
going by in the road calls out
"Good morning" or "Good luck".

No use of early rising:
as useless is thy watching.
No traveller bestows
a word of blessing on the grass,
nor minds it as he goes.

Climb the stair
manfully, and sing
a short song on each step of the stair.

It is not an arduous duty.
Eblis was hard, not Zion.

Inditing A Good Matter

I find nothing to say,
I am heavy as lead.
I take small satisfaction
in anything I have said.

Evangelists want your assent,
be it cringing, or idle, or eager.
God shrugs. We taste dismay,
as sharp as vinegar.

He shrugs. How can He care
what *billets-doux* we send Him,
how much we applaud? Such coxcombs
inclined to commend Him!

My heart had been inditing
a good matter. My tongue
was the pen of a ready writer
who had been writing too long.

Whoever supposes his business
is to commend and bless
is due for this comeuppance:
feeling it less and less.

But I find something to say.
I pump it out, heavy as lead:
"Buoy me up out of the shadow
of your ramparts overhead."

Like one of those vanished performers
on an afternoon-matinée console,
I arise:
          "Admit to your rock
this ready, this shriven, soul."

The Creature David

The disposings of the heart in man,
and the answer of the tongue...
Not the domain of any
main poet's song;

not the halcyon, the mid-ocean range
where Ceteosaurus spouts, and Christopher Smart
numbers the streaks of the mollusc, where
the Spaniard is challenged for the Main
comradely, and Drake takes on the world,
a hirsute pirate. None of this
is documented history, it is not
fastidious, but dreadnought David's song.

Speech murmurs, and is always
forked, but this is song.
Nothing in this is talked.

There goe the shippes; there is
that Leviathan, whom Thou hast made
to play therein

upon the harp.

Saw I Never The Righteous Forsaken

I have been young, and now am old:

but I never saw Mr Worth
denied all reputation,
nor Mrs Worth and the children
go begging in the long run.

Reputations have
what seems when you get to my age
a shortish innings at best.
Remember the champion jockeys?
How many? From how far back?

"He shall bring forth thy
righteousness as the light,
the judgement as the noonday."

Banking on posterity
is an unwise investment.
Cold comfort, the little Worths!
Perpetual false dawn!

But merit is ascertainable as daylight;
unarguable justice follows
as certainly as noon ensues from dawn.

The Elect

Battle of Britain Sunday, RAF Gatow, Berlin

In their conventicles
stone-built or notional
they have withdrawn
from the life of the nation, or
have been excluded from it.

Strident, unaccommodating,
inelegant, sometimes smug,
they have despaired, and exchange
their Hosannas with each other.

An enclosed subculture,
they speak of such a one
no one has heard of, as
a guide to their devotions.

They comprehended, as
no others did, the fate
of the burned-up, scorched and screaming
sergeant-pilots:

as
gold in the furnace has He
tried them, and received them
as a burnt offering.

Luftwaffe pilots, also?
Don't fuss me. Yes, of course.

They shall shine and run to and fro
like sparks among the stubble,

for though in the sight of men and in
the sight of the unwise they seem to die,

they are in peace and

shall judge the nations.

"The just die young, and are happy."

What sort of a nation is this,
bows its sleek head to these
outrageous obsequies,

born of a happiness in
the ghetto of the elect?

The Zodiac

It won't stand up to the light;
disgraceful, though

They fought from heaven, the stars in their courses fought
against Sisera, sang
Deborah, and Barak the son of Abinoam sang,
but Deborah in those days, saying:

Star-crossed, ill-starred, oh ill-starred Sisera!

Infirmity no doubt
of our nature, that we guess at
this nonsensical band in
the heavens dispensing justice.

But that much should be allowed us.
Misfortune undoubtedly strikes
unequally, and to the worst
worldling one would not deny
the chance of blaming, rather
than God, a star-struck Nature.

In this way the sad Lorine
Niedecker, to explain
the ill luck of her father and mother,
remarked not once but often
Mars rising in Pisces, if
that is possible;
                                    she,
raised and persisting in
a watery, piscatorial
district of Wisconsin,

assured the elemental
energies must have some
relation to the cosmos:
a God-enforced decorum.

"Just You Wait!"

To justify God's ways to man
like Eliphaz the Temanite
is a presumptuous folly;
it cannot be done.

Until the hurt comes I shall glorify
God on account of the ostrich,
hippopotamus, elephant,
crocodile, and whale.

(Zoological marvels:
King Edward the Seventh's racehorse,
his vertebrae fused together
from carrying a weight of jockeys.)

Who is confident though Jordan
rushes against his mouth,
who also lieth under the shady tree
in the covert of the reede, and fennes?

This is a riddle-me-ree.
"Hippopotamus" is the answer.
Until the hurt comes, and after,
play piously riddle-me-ree.

It comes, it is on its way, that hurting business;
it shall not be my affair until it comes.

Bowing The Head

Importunate for attention,
hanging around
the ante-rooms of Eternity,
the position of prayer, it must be
allowed, lacks dignity.

How much more, if it is not
hanging around so much as
hawking our goods, and the claim
we have by them, each howling
the loved one's, the needed one's, Name.

It is the position of love,
and which of us has not known it?
Lothario cannot gainsay it:
virility is the more
abject, the more we display it.

So, how to be manly in prayer?
"Hawking about for attention..."
It is a pungent phrase.
Getting down on your knees,
remember it all your days.

Widower

That sneaky Thomas Cranmer!
Turns out he had two
illicit marriages. One
cost him his fellowship at Cambridge.

Whence Matrimony, his
doing
in 1549:
"a remedy against
fornication". (Other things also.)

Which makes ungrateful
sense for those
whose penis is a sacred member.

Poor Thomas Cranmer, his
doings in the dark!

"As Isaac and Rebecca gave
        A pattern chaste and kind,
To make domestic burthens light
        By taking mutual share,
        When we asunder part,
        It gives us inward pain."

It is for you like tonsured
Ronsard, less
the bedmate you miss than the faithful,
the sometimes spitfire friend,

whatever the small hours' stress.

Master & Man

(Proverbs 19.22)

Chaste and kind... "a pattern"
(Isaac and Rebecca)
"chaste and kind". Such words
What we have done to you
both long ago and lately....

For "chaste", read "pure"; for "kind"
("The desire of a man is his kindness")
read, "What is desired in a man
is loyalty." Biddable man!

My lord, my liege lord, my dear
lord, what I desire is
my own and not your kindness.

A poor man is better than a liar,
dear my lord, suppose the
desire of a man is his kindness;

extended also
to the unthankful,
whose kindness is as a morning cloud
and as the early dew it goeth away,

milord.

Levity

What is man that you should weigh
the gravamen of his "grievous unto me"?

The weight of his sins he must
profess intolerable;
"imponderable" comes nearer.

For he knows them light as a feather;
changeable, like history or the weather.

"Laïs, boy-prostitute, wife"
(he addresses them), "were we not
all on the side of Life?"

The beam kicks: lift-off Man,
no counterweight in the pan,

no peise, no pondering, no
poise, no *avoirdupois*,

no slug of compassionate lead
to weigh him saved or convicted,

soars into and over the sunrise.
The angels are all eyes.

Oh slender, eternally youthful
balloonist, what you have missed!

For there He is, steadily weighing
your airy, your weightiest, saying.

Witness

Bearing and giving are different, it appears.

In the latter case (constrained)
one supposes, or may suppose,
a judge and a jury. In the case of

bearing

witness, there is a load
that has to be discharged
in physical fact, the weight
on the grieving shoulders
thankfully hefted off,
a sack into the shadows of God's barton.

No judge, no jury, but one,
that one incalculable, His
authority established by no statute.

"Come, O my guilty brethren, come,
Groaning beneath your load of sin."

We bear like a weight in the gut
witness, a load that
must be evacuated
in the hedge-bottom or elsewhere.

Our Lady

The sea is all that they say: it wreaks death one way only;
it neither begins nor ends, nor ever suspends its motions;
indifferent as to racial stock and
era, it drowns
or does not drown, impartially, godlike in this,
not to be walked on.
                                        One who
walked on the sea, though briefly,
walked also alone under olives also briefly,
seldom alone and always.
                                                This his mother,
crude-painted odalisque, holds in her left hand
a seaport sacked, in her right hand a votive ship
tiny among trumperies, cheap mirrors.

                                                        She the recalcitrant sailor's
one and one only reached-after landfall, but under
an interdict he hymns, he worships instead,
and plumes with his perjured feathers
of spume and inconsequent waterspout, the faithless
indifferent non-god, Ocean.

The Ironist

"Sacred? or sacrosanct?
or sanctimonious, even?
Suppose you chose these topics
(which, you will say, chose you),
hoping to escape
the debilitating scope
of your kind in your time and place:

irony."

It is Lord Haw-haw speaking;
it is Mephistophilis speaking,
the syphilitic; it is
Germany speaking.

A masterly ironist
of history knows
his subject inside out;
his dry wit drying out
a sop of sentiment from
the cerements of the West.

Lover of the mephitic,
of fog and stink,
his natural haunt the road by the chemicals plant,

his elegant strong suit
is tacit and total carnage:
the Devil's work, whose mark
(frivolity and distraction)
is on this page also

as on the best we can do.

"Thou Art Near At Hand, O Lord"

Or: *They are come near me that*
persecute me of malice.

How near was near? Were their camels
cropping his starveling pastures?

Or were they behind the skyline,
though they might be his "nearest and dearest"?
Were they never in fact (though in truth)
shouldering for house-room?

It is thus with words on the page:
"Mephistophilis" and "mephitic"
are more nearly juxtaposed
than two that are side by side.

Moreover, space is encoded
to signify lapses of time.
(One verse-line under another;
this one *after* that one.)

The nearness of God is known as
an aching absence:
the room the reception-desk
cannot locate nor account for,

in a fictitious or
analogous space that does not
answer to or observe
the parameters of Newton,

any more than a page of verse does.

The Nosegay

The roses of irony blossom
floridly on the trellis
of inexperience crossed with
a need for the fell and certain.

Seeing that irony is
the adolescent's defence,
"An end to irony!" means
death to most of our lyrics.

The objection to the God
of Islam and of Judah,
"He lacks a sense of humour",
means, He is not ironical,
He is not a lyrical God.

He does not come and go;
He is not glimpsed in gaps of
time. Alas, it is clear that
He claims to be omnipresent,
and had better be thus acknowledged.

He has His sense of fun
surely; He has even
(as we see it, who wait on deathbeds)
a mordant wit.

It is the bite of the wit
mauls our sense of humour.

Lyrists may proclaim their
intermittent visions;
ironists, their protective
clothing; but the surgeon

of Islam and of Judah
makes His incisions
justly, and He is not
deprecating about it.

Stepping along the Turl,
selecting a buttonhole
half mauve, half mustard-yellow,
what God and what men you malign!

Gripping Serial

Man fought against beasts, and won;
Man fought against priests, and won;
Man fought against kings, and won;
Now he fights the Collective.

This drivel is still believed.

Man fought against beasts;
Man fought against Man, and still does;

And there's the end of the series.

I Have Said, Ye Are Gods

And so you might have been:
a groaning light, a light that risked eclipse
and underwent it. Oh
luminaries, oh
sun and moon and stars of a low-browed heaven,

Enlighteners,

Captain Cook was the best of you,
bashing his bowsprit through
the gap between ice-floe and
a bruised cloud-ceiling, past
Bering's best, and may even have died for his friends.

But in twenty centuries,
not under the cove and whelm
of the *tsunami*, nor
splintered upon the wakes
of any nation's navy, breaks
the light that saves.

He maketh men to be
of one mind in an house,

and ye princes shall fall as one of the common sort.

David Dancing

Infrequently, dreams are heavenly
How if the caustic "Thou
dreamer!" excoriate those
hagridden by what, in a sleep
we learn to dread, comes often?

For dreams, most dreams, are hell.
Sundry authorities
exhort us to "come to terms",
get used to our hells, distrust
the dull or brilliant daylight.

Neither to move nor console,
David dances before
the Ark. And the Ark is not
the dance, but what the dance
honours and accedes to.

Neither to move nor console
he dances, not in a dream
but exceptionally wakeful
in a recurrent morning.

Dancing Measures

Noah drunken, taking
his daughters in bed; a common,
seldom avowed occurrence.

How then for the dance, that is always
a self-abuser, glassed
in the pond of its own procedures?

The wrath of God! Yet Dance's
habitual incest seems
not to call down thunders.

Wrong! The penalty is
imposed in intimate places:
a rhythm imposed by no
more than proclivity, yet
prohibitively binding.

Measures, the prison of measures:
rumtitum, tumtitum, rum.
You know of a worse crucifixion?

What drunken stupor or
generative torpor sets
fingers or feet to tapping like Astaire?

Sometimes the drink implants it;
sometimes, God-induced, it
shakes free and runs loose, if the dancer's
executive will dispose it, to high meadows.

Being Angry With God

"Anger, yes. But God is God",
the impious Pakistani
explained to V.S. Naipaul.
"God is not like people."

Profound: God is not like people.

Shallow: He ought to be.

Indifference, if you can
manage it (youth can),
disposes of God well enough.

Imran runs up to bowl. The Rajput palaces
live not as art but as the youth
Imran, accelerating, is on the verge of losing.

Even with people, what did
anger ever dispose of?
It ties you in, like love.

Thanks to an undevout Muslim,
we recognize anger with God is
one more way to own Him.

The ex-Christian exclaims:
"But my angers amount to something!"
It is not at all clear that they do,

as Imran Khan
turns and begins his run:
poetry in motion.

The motion is unforgiving;
so is the poetry; so
(unless it is tempered) the Judgement.

The Comforter

St. Patrick bound unto himself
the Trinity, but showed his practical sainthood
by playing down the third
member of the triad. No
anxious souls would be won by
that vaporous Holy Ghost.

"The whirling wind's tempestuous shocks"
registers Patrick's obeisance, but
no one is taken in, no one prays to the wind.

And indeed He is the strangest
of the Three Persons,
the most estranged.

For the Holy Ghost is nakedly a ghost.
Father and Son may be masks
compassionately adapted
to our capacities, but
Person is not *persona* and
the Ghost is a ghost, no fiction.

Integration, fulfilment
have nothing to do with this Person;
cure, or harmony – nothing
like that is intended.

Invasion is His note:
disintegration.
A wind from the outside corners
of the human map;
disorienting;

His strangeness for the comfort
of those not at home in the grid.

*Cannibals**

As if to take in ocean
through a needle's eye,
a sundial divines
not why light moves, but when;

when, and how. He moves
now. And perhaps He loves us.
He moves in any case.
We trace, not chart, His passage,

like Uruguayan, defiled
prop-forwards and blind-side flankers,
iced up in the Andes,
cannibals, knowing Him near.

My horne shalt thou exalt
like the horne of an unicorne.

Presence, the nearness, is
the needle's eye;
not to make any more
proof of it, the trial.

Pray to the Holy Spirit, Let
not the most polluted
translation impede the witness:
ram's horn of unvarying plenty!

* "The Old Christians", a Rugby football team from Montevideo, was isolated in a wrecked aircraft from October to December 1972.

Woe Unto Thee!

Compunction at presumption
is a sentiment
conspicuous by its absence
from the college of prophets.

David the King, Isaiah,
Micah – what
regal or less than regal
prerogative gave them the right
to be so unforgiving?

Choked with the god, or blinded
by arrogance,
they were – by what right? – lifted
above being fair-minded.

Had they not thought of circumstance
extenuating?

"He that is free of sin, let him
cast the first stone." Had they,
the fulminating,
nothing to atone for?

Baldly declarative,
their comminations live
on in the Scriptures like
an unacknowledged toothache,
bruising and assertive.

The nerve sings, and so long as
it sings, presumption calls for
no halter of compunction.

Kingship

It would have been because
they smelled so bad,
that the scriptural nomads and
city-dwellers made
so much of oils, of resinous
exudations
of Gilead; and we,
if our stick of deodorant is
jammed, what indignity!
The feel of that, and the fear

unfelt by the cheerful, the fearless
non-conforming whom
we hate accordingly with
olfactory revulsion.

The sweat of honest labour is
too honest for our noses.
And of dishonest?

Joy unto thee, if thou canst
muster a patience beyond
"The time will come." It will not.
Idyllic earth where the hay smells of the dream
in Samuel Palmer's Shoreham
will not, it is certain, surface
in history, though a few
institutions hint of it: for instance

"the Lord's anointed",

sweating beneath his robes,
holding the orb and sceptre,
who would have been happier in
the malodorousness of Goodwood;

and over him Another
enthroned in majesty
"no sweat".

Ordinary God

"Do you believe in a God
who can change the course of events
on earth?"
"No, just
the ordinary one."
A laugh,
but not so stupid: events
He does not, it seems, determine
for the most part. Whether He could
is not to the point; it is not
stupid to believe in
a God who mostly abjures.

The ordinary kind
of God is what one believes in
so implicitly that
it is only with blushes or
bravado one can declare,
"I believe"; caught as one is
in the ambush of personal history, so
harried, so distraught.

The ordinary kind
of undeceived believer
expects no prompt reward
from an ultimately faithful
but meanwhile preoccupied landlord.

Nashville Mornings

Saint Cecilia:
                    between
man as vehicle traversed
by constant, by unchanging
biological forces; and
his actions as reactions
solely to speedy changes –
where is the third term? Is it
what in the ghetto of letters
we least can stomach: Noise,
the appalling Rock and Country?
The damnable steel guitar?

Cruising Canadian
coaches pause
by the patios of the stars,

expensive silences, Olympus,
Arcturus, a loft above tundra
built by and out of
clang, twang, nasalsong
and corybantes? There is precedent:

at Stonehenge, ululations,
the nuptial hymn a disco.

Dawdling the Franklin road
Ontario plates;
gardeners, sprinklers,
                                Elvis
his platinum-plated Rolls
garaged in splendour. Old
Etonian freshman gawped
along with the rest. There is
spring on the world, and all the
time in the yawning

road for pleasurable
memories, anticipations
of strum and drum. The form is
a rhythmical suck. The air-brakes
ease from the sidewalk gently:
Homes of the Stars!

"thought I would like to
if it's all
right. On my way to Chicago.
You knew me when I was two."
Youth on the road.

Graze the glass bowl, however
musically, the fish
in the fishbowl flick their tails
once, and are gone.

Flaw and withdraw, the
exquisite
accomplishments of flautists,
is that an achievement?

If we inhabit a gap
between the departure of gods and
their necessary return,

their absence is a salience
no doubt, as with
Chinese ceramics also,
a scrape on the ineffable. It
makes sense. Makes enough?

"What I had known, no one had known.
What I had seen, no one had seen."
A man in love with silence, in
terror of silence, and in love with that:
tundra, snow-oceans. Rasp or whisper,
the wind outside.
"A silence fell between them."

Cecilia, her music
confined in its operations
to a metaphysical annex,
irks on Nashville mornings.

Brilliance

Some virtue in
                    the ultimate
lack of emphasis: "Gods
                    or it may be one God moves
about us in bright air."

Not for you. You were brilliant. You always meant to be
        that.
You were, and still are at times.

Brilliance, still you want it
impenitently. Truth, oh as for....

You were not in love with the world
or never for long, and only with bits of it:
the usual bits. Trees in a forest? Not often.

Better in a vicarage garden
in the fens, a shelf of cedar
above two deck-chairs, untenanted then and for ever
at four o'clock of a summer afternoon.

But that was not brilliant enough, or not for long.

Diamonds, and still the blonde deserves
        them,
a whole tiara, festoons on the sky at
        night

or on the white page, black facets;
impenitence, a diamond in itself,
unbreakable, breaking others.

The sinne of Judah is written
with a pen of yron,
and with the point of a diamond it is graven
on the tables of their hearts.

Constant, but only in
the impenitent pursuit
of self-destruction – has
that little earned the garlands
of cadence and clear colour?

The alcoholic's delusion
that he controls his habit,
the warrior, his –
is this to be esteemed and
heroically lamented

in Dylan Thomas, in
a broken Coriolanus?

If to be free of delusion
is the worst delusion of all,
are we to save our applause
for those whose delusions are noblest;
for instance, loving the world?

Granted, the noble is
unarguable, known as
soon as apprehended;
still, Delusion limes his
limp nets also for eagles.

Brilliance is known in
what the tired wing, though
it never so crookedly towers,
wins at last into: air
diamond-clear, unemphatic.

Brilliance, then, is noble;
not in the subject but
in what the subject attains to:
a metaphysical, not
in the first place human, property.

"Can you tell the down from the up?"
The unthinkable answer: No.
God moves about us, and
brilliance is His preferred
supernal way of moving.

If I Take The Wings Of The Morning

taking off at dawn
to circle *ultima thule,*

threading the splendours between
ice and pearl cloud cover,

God is not only also
there, but signally there,

who made the heavens skilfully,
who made the great lights
with a strong hand and a strained-out arm,

who brought forth clouds from the end of the world
and sent forth lightnings with rain
and out of His treasuries high winds.

When those who keep us in prison
ask of us mirth in our hang-ups
with "Sing us a song of Zion",
what can we sing or say
under the mourning willows
of a common suffering in
the river-meadows of Babel?

It is our lingo utters us, not we.
Our native tongue, our endowment,
determines what we can say.
And who endowed us?

Speak if you cannot sing.
Utter with appropriate shudders
the extremities of God's arctic
where all the rivers are frozen,

and how He tempers our exile
with an undeserved planting of willows.